HOW TO SELL YOUR CAR FOR MORE THAN IT'S WORTH

A GREGORY PUBLICATION

HOW TO SELL YOUR CAR FOR MORE THAN IT'S WORTH

A GREGORY PUBLICATION

Gregory Publications
Post Office Box 796
Rosemead, California 91770

ISBN: 0-917224-04-3
Library of Congress Catalog Card No. 77-73616

cover photo by Louis Vega
cartoon artwork by Mike Dooley

Although many sellers treat potential buyers like "top dogs", they usually feel like a fire hydrant as the purchaser drives away with their car. To these sellers, I dedicate this book.

Contents:

Introduction

Does it seem to you that it's always somebody else that sells his car for top dollar? Have you ever sold a car, and thought back on how you gave it away? Well, you're not alone. Millions of used cars are sold every year....Some for more than they're worth, a larger number for what they're worth, and even a larger number for less than they're worth. In the pages to follow, I'm going to show you how to join those who sell their cars for *more* than they're worth.

Between the ages of 17 and 21, I bought and re-sold over 250 cars and trucks. During this time I learned what it took for a car to bring the highest price, and I became an expert on writing result-producing advertisements. On my twenty-first birthday I went to work for a large Chevrolet dealer in the Los Angeles area. For the first three months I was assigned to the new car sales department. I did well, but I couldn't keep my eyes from wandering to the section of the dealership that fascinated me the most...the used car lot.

When a position on this lot finally became open, I made it evident that I wanted to be the one to fill it. "I'll give you a try," said the used car manager, "but if you don't produce I won't be able to keep you."

I felt right at home with those fabulous used cars. No two were alike, and each had its very own selling point. I secured my new position by selling more cars than anyone else in the dealership my first month. The thing I was most fascinated with was the methods in which the used cars were reconditioned. Although I thought I knew all the tricks to making a car look its best, I felt humbled when I saw my used car manager at work. He was more than a professional automobile man — he was an artist. He could take the scroungiest car in town and turn it into a showpiece.

During my first week on the used car lot, a 1966 Chevrolet Impala coupe was towed in by a repossession agency. The transmission was bad, it needed a fair amount of body work, and the the interior looked as though dogs had been living in it. After examining it, I asked my manager if he were going to junk it. "Of course not," he replied. "I'll have it on the front line next week." I figured that the only way he could recondition this car would be to jack up the radiator cap and drive another car underneath it.

About a week later I came in to work the afternoon shift, and, just like the man had told me, this car was sitting on the front line. It looked so good that at first I didn't recognize it as being the same car. That same evening, a man and his wife came onto the lot, and their eyes were captured by this car. "Boy! Whoever had this car certainly took good care of it!" said the husband as he walked around it. "How much are you asking?" One hour later, the couple drove their new purchase home.

"Did we make any money on the car?" I asked my manager.

"About $600," he replied. From this time on, I became infatuated with the reconditioning processes employed by automobile dealers.

In the years to follow I was to become sales manager, and these responsibilities were to become mine. When the new car sales were down and the trade-ins were few,

I would have to buy cars in order to keep the used car lot well-stocked. Although there were wholesale auto auctions that I could attend, and independent automobile wholesalers that were located nearby, I always found that I could buy better cars — at better prices — from the private party sellers.

Searching the classified sections of the local newspapers, I found plenty of persons selling their cars for *less* than they were worth. Luckily for me, only a person familiar with automobile reconditioning practices could recognize the true values of these cars. I would purchase as many as 25 automobiles per month from these sellers, and the profit on each would range from $500 to $1500. If the persons whom I had purchased these cars from had the information that I'm about to give you, they would have this extra money instead of the automobile dealer.

1

Mechanical Reconditioning

Major engine problems

I don't have any secrets on how to make a worn-out or burned-up engine run like new for only a few dollars. If you have an automobile in dire need of major engine work, ask yourself this question: "What is the highest price that my car could bring if the engine were in good condition?" If this amount is $1,000 or less, then I would have to tell you to save yourself the aggravation of having this work done, and to sell the car "as-is".

I have a friend who once had a rough '65 Mustang with a blown engine. He called to ask me where he could locate a used engine for the car so he could sell it. "How much are you going to ask for the car once it's running?", I asked.

"I hope that I can get $600," he said.

"How much are you willing to pay for an engine?"

"I'd like to find one for about $300..." he answered.

"Don't take the trouble of fixing it...," I said. "Place an ad in the paper stating it needs engine work and price it at $475."

"That's more than it's worth," he said. "I don't think I can get it, but I'll give it a try." My friend advertised his car the following week-end, and received $475.

In every city there are a vast number of "back yard" mechanics who are always looking for fixer-uppers, and they may be willing to pay the price you ask. Major engine work can give you a major headache, so it's best to pass it on to the next guy. Again, this applies to older, lower priced automobiles.

If you have a late model car, or have decided to have your engine repaired before trying to sell it, then you might consider having a short block installed. When you have the original engine rebuilt, many unforseen problems can arise, and the low price which you were first quoted can take a tremendous jump upward.

By purchasing a short block, you'll know what you're spending from the onset, with no surprises to follow later. Watch for specials on short blocks in your local newspaper. You'll find that the independent shops will offer the lowest prices. (These specials are usually advertised in the classified sections of newspapers under the heading of "Automobile Parts & Accessories".)

Common Engine Problems

Tune-ups. When an engine runs rough, you'll usually discover that faulty or dirty spark plugs are the culprits. You can be sure of this if the engine tends to miss severely during acceleration. Tune-ups don't come cheaply these days, so if spark plugs alone will cure your car's problems, then there isn't any need for replacing anything else.

When I was buying and selling cars on my own, every car I purchased received a set of "reconditioned" plugs. Although most mechanics scoff at those using these plugs,

I tell you now that they'll last nearly as long as the new ones. These plugs can be purchased in a package of eight from most discount department stores. The cost: about $2 per set or 25¢ each. That's much better than paying $1.75 apiece for new ones. Installing spark plugs is a very simple procedure, and you should be able to complete the installation within 30 minutes.

If you don't want to bother with this work yourself, or if your engine needs a major tune-up, then watch your local paper for tune-up specials, or find a local shop which specializes in tuning engines for a minimal price.

Engine Noises. Any potential buyer looking at your car is going to raise the hood while the engine is running, and any noises that your engine may have will sound much louder with the hood open. Most buyers cannot tell the difference in sound between a good and bad engine. Because of this lack of mechanical knowledge, the slightest, most insignificant noise can easily queer a sale.

Valves. I've lost many a sale simply because of minor valve noises. If your engine's valves need adjusting, then please have these adjustments made before you attempt to sell your car. The cost is relatively low, and a good garage should be able to complete the adjustment within a couple of hours.

Fan belts. Screeching fan belts can be cured in one of two ways — 1. By tightening them. (Do this only if they need tightening. If the belts are tightened too tight, they'll eventually damage other parts.) 2. By applying "lube stick" to the belts' surfaces. (This can be purchased at any parts or hardware store. It generally has the appearance of a large crayon.) Applying lube stick won't eliminate the squeaking noise permanently, but it will keep the belts quiet for a week or two while you're trying to sell your car.

Muffler or exhaust noises. If your car needs a muffler, tailpipe, or exhaust pipe gaskets, then have them replaced. A loud exhaust always tends to make an engine sound as though it's not running properly. (VW owners: If you've installed a new, non-factory exhaust system on your car, you'll stand a much better chance of receiving top dollar if you'll take this contraption off and replace it with the *original* equipment. Although this performance-type exhaust may make your car run better, it will be an eyesore to the average prospect.)

Heat Control Valve. The heat control valve is generally connected to the exhaust manifold, and on the V8 engines is located on the right hand exhaust manifold. When the engine is cold, this valve diverts the flow of the hot exhaust gases, passing them through special sections of the intake manifold. This helps to vaporize the fuel passing through the cold intake manifold, and makes a cold engine run smoother. Once the engine has warmed up, the valve opens to permit the gases to flow unrestricted through the exhaust pipe. Should this valve become stuck in either position, the car's performance will be affected.

This valve is automatically controlled by a thermostatic spring and a counterweight. The operation of the heat control valve can be checked by moving the counterweight the full course of its travel. If it seems to be stuck, a generous application of penetrating oil will usually set it free.

The most common malfunction of the heat control valve is the breakage of the thermostatic spring. When this occurs, the butterfly-type valve inside the manifold flops around freely, making an irritating rattling noise. If you think that your car might have this problem, you can quickly confirm it by moving the counterweight with a screwdriver while the engine is running. If, by moving this part, the rattling noises cease, then you'll know for sure that this part is bad. You can have it repaired at a small cost at your local garage.

The Transmission

Until I began working for an automobile dealership, I was under the impression that it was impossible to have an automatic transmission rebuilt for anything less than $400. You can imagine how surprised I was when I discovered three local shops that would rebuild an automatic transmission — on almost any make of car — for a cost ranging from $100 to a guranteed maximum of $145. This price included *installation* and *free pick-up and delivery* of the car from my lot! I bragged about this price to the owner of a local used car lot, and he thought I might be paying too much!

You're probably wondering why many dealers sublet transmission repair for their used cars when they have the facilities to rebuild transmissions themselves, so I'll explain...

Department relationships

Although a dealer's service department and used car lot may be under the same roof, they are two *separate* departments. Each has its own manager, and both must answer for their department's profit. The service department, therefore, must show a fair profit when doing work on the used car manager's cars, so it extends only a small discount on parts and labor. Also, a screaming retail customer receives higher priority and faster service than does a screaming used car manager.

Labor

I believe that the average labor charge, at present, is about $12 per hour. Most service departments divide this amount with their mechanics 50/50. Therefore, when you receive a bill showing a $120 charge for 8 hours of labor, $60 goes to the mechanic who performed the repair, and the other $60 goes to the service department.

But did the repair actually take eight hours to complete? Although one mechanic may be able to rebuild a transmission in four hours, it might take another mechanic 12 hours to do the same job. In order to compensate for the wide variation between different mechanics' speed, service departments use an automobile repair "rate book" which sets a limit on the amount of time that a mechanic

can charge for each task he performs. Naturally, the mechanic will "flag" this maximum amount of time on the repair order. (To flag means to attach a gum-labeled strip showing the mechanic's employee number and the number of hours that he spent making a repair. A carbon copy of this label is retained by the mechanic for payroll purposes.)

Please don't think that I'm criticizing the mechanics for charging for the maximum time allotted. I've seen mechanics flag 65 or 70 hours worth of time in a 40-hour week, and I'm happy for them because they must work like hell to accomplish this much work. I've also seen some of the slower mechanics work a full 40 hours, and only be able to flag 20 hours. (Most mechanics employed by automobile dealers work solely on commission. No work, no pay; much work, much pay.)

Why are the dealers entitled to half of the labor charges? Because they furnish the facilities, the advertising, the customers, and the service manager and service advisors who advise and pamper the retail customers.

Many of the independent transmission shops don't pay their mechanics as well as do the auto dealers. (If they do, they take a much smaller cut for themselves.) Because their mechanics specialize only in transmission work, the repair is accomplished in a shorter time, and this labor savings is passed on to the customer. The independent shops generally offer a shorter guarantee period than does the larger dealer, but this enables them to offer a more competitive price. (The quality of work is usually equal.)

Parts

Although an auto dealer's parts department is usually considered part of the service department, it, too, has its own manager. When you take your car in to be repaired, not only do you pay top dollar for the labor, but you also pay full retail for the parts. (Which, unfortunately, have a very high mark-up.) The dealer must insist on a high profit from his parts because he has several employees working behind the counter, a parts pick-up and delivery driver and truck, a cashier, a parts manager, and a huge inventory of slow-moving parts which he must always have on hand. In other words, the dealer has a large *overhead*.

The independent shops have little overhead where parts are concerned. When a part is needed, a quick phone call to a local supplier sends the part on its way. The parts used by the independent shops are generally manufactured by local firms, and aren't nearly as expensive as the "genuine factory" parts which are sold by the dealerships. The independent shops also use rebuilt parts when available, and although the large dealerships may occasionally use rebuilt parts, they will add a large mark-up. My neighbor owns a factory which rebuilds transmission torque converters. The average converter wholesales for approximately $20, yet sells for $65 over a parts counter. A rip-off? No, just business.

I have gone into great depth about major garages vs. the independents, but I believe the advantages of dealing with an independent shop hold especially true where automatic transmissions are concerned. (When I say independent shops, I *don't* mean *franchised* shops.)

If your car's transmission is failing, check with a local used car dealer. Have him recommend you to the shop he uses. Unless the transmission in your car works properly, you're going to have trouble selling it...at any price! This is one thing that the average backyard mechanic will not attempt to fix. I have purchased many automobiles — with bad transmissions — for a helluva lot less than they were worth. If these cars would've had mechanical problems other than the transmissions, they would have been sold long before I had the opportunity to see them.

Brakes

"That Ford Maverick you sold me last night needs brakes desperately, and I wanna know what you're gonna to do about it?" said the irate customer.

"I guess I'll have to include accident and health insurance in your contract...", I replied.

"Weak brakes? They always seemed O.K. to me..."

How many times have you heard someone say, "I just spent $150 for a brake job"? Maybe you've spent this much yourself in the past, but chances are that you spent too much. If your car needs brakes, watch for specials in the newspaper. Advertisements for most automotive needs are generally found in the sports section.

Don't fall for the ads which show a charge for the labor alone, or you'll get stung with a high parts bill. A complete brake reline job should cost no more than $45, or $60 if your car has front disc brakes. This price should include "turning" the drums and discs. Many times, a garage will try to sell you on the idea that your car needs all of the wheel cylinders rebuilt. Unless your car is using brake fluid and there is a physical trace of fluid leaking from the wheel cylinders, don't have them rebuilt. If one of the wheel cylinders is definitely leaking, then have only that one particular cylinder repaired.

If you own a later model automobile and you are having brake work done for the first time, chances are that only your front brakes need replacing. Don't be fooled when a mechanic examines your rear brakes and starts talking "percentages". As used car manager, I don't know how many times a mechanic would tell me that one of my used car's rear brakes had "less than 50% lining remaining", and needed replacing. Bull. Usually a car must travel at *least* 25,000 miles before half of the brake lining is worn in the rear.

Therefore, when a mechanic tells you that there's "less than 50% of the lining left", he is actually telling you that you have "less than 25,000 miles to travel before you'll need to replace the linings". That's the same as a doctor examining a 40-year-old man and telling him that he only has 40 more years to live!

Emergency brakes

Nothing is more aggravating than an inoperative emergency brake. Although a simple adjustment will cure this problem, many owners neglect to make the repair because there's a "park" setting on the transmission, or, if the car is a standard shift, putting it in gear when the engine is off will keep it from rolling. Any prospective buyer who looks at your car is going to test this brake, so be sure that it's adjusted properly.

Tires

There's so much competition in the tire field that an individual can purchase tires for just about the same price as can a volume dealer. All that I can tell you is to watch for specials, spend a couple extra dollars for whitewalls, and have them balanced properly.

If your tires are in fair shape, it would probably be wise to have them rotated. Front tires will always show wear on the outside edge of the tread, and the average buyer usually can't wait to tell you that your car's front wheels are out of alignment.

Directional signals, headlamps, etc.

Every prospective buyer will check the operation of your car's lights, so be sure they're working. If your directional signals blink on only one side of the car, this generally indicates a bad bulb on one side. If neither signal blinks, then you probably have either a bad flasher or a bad bulb on both sides of your car. These items can be replaced in a few minutes. Although they are only minor problems, too many minor problems display a lack of maintenance.

Lubricate!

Although you may maintain a lubrication schedule, you'll probably have some items which haven't seen any lubrication since your car was new.

The hood hinge is the most commonly overlooked yet most crucial part. Without proper lubrication, the hinge will begin to bind, requiring extra effort from the person opening the hood. Eventually, these dry hinges can break or cause the hood to bend. If your hood seems to be somewhat stiff, put several drops of oil on these hinges and work the hood up and down until it operates smoothly and all squeaks disappear.

While the oil can is out, lubricate the door and trunk hinges. Also, lube stick applied to their latch mechanisms will insure easier releasing and closing.

Difficult-to-turn ignition switches, door locks, glove box locks, and trunk locks should be lubricated with graphite. It's always embarrasing when a prospective buyer must struggle to turn a key.

Oil Change

If the oil in your engine is dirty, spend a few dollars for an oil change and a new oil filter. The first step a prospect will take after opening your car's hood will be to pull out the dipstick to check the color of the oil, so be a step ahead by having clean oil.

If your car is equipped with an automatic transmission, you may run across a prospect who will remove the transmission fluid dipstick and smell it. Don't let this shake you. In some cases, a burnt odor can indicate transmission problems, but most persons don't know what they're looking for, and are only trying to impress someone by going through this "smelling" motion.

I once had a prospective buyer who would smell the transmission dipstick on every car that I showed him. When he finally decided on a particular car, he asked me to take a look at his trade-in. He watched me as I opened the hood on his car, so I thought I'd humor him by smelling *his* car's transmission dipstick. He eyes were studying my moves so intently that I thought I'd go another step further and *taste* the fluid. I then nodded my head and shut the hood. A few minutes later, the young man and I were in my office discussing monthly payments. "Do you want to buy the car?" I asked.

"Let me look at it one more time...," he replied.

My office overlooked the lot, and I remained seated as I watched my prospect begin to re-examine the car he was considering purchasing. He didn't realize that I could see him frantically removing the car's transmission dipstick and tasting its fluid. I don't know how many swipes he made at the dipstick with his tongue, but the edges of his mouth and the spaces between his teeth were bright red with fluid when he returned to the office. "By the way...," I said to him as he seated himself, "I tasted the fluid in that car myself when it came in a few days ago, and it's fine."

"Yeah...," he replied, "I just now double-checked it and it seems o.k. to me, too."

2

Your Car's Exterior

On several occasions I have sold a car merely on its appearance, with the customer never once starting the engine until the car was his. This doesn't occur very often, but it certainly proves that the outward appearance of an automobile plays the most important role in making a sale. Although your car may run better than new, most potential buyers will not even be interested in driving it unless the exterior is appealing. Let us now begin from the ground up...

Tires

Nothing looks worse on a car than mis-matched tires. Since many car owners buy only two tires at a time, this isn't an uncommon sight. Thin whitewalls up front, double-striped whitewalls on the rear, etc. There's an inexpensive cure for this problem, and — although it has been around for a long time — few people know of it.

This cure is known as "tire rings" or "toppers". These marvelous items can be used to correct almost any tire appearance problems. Although the tire must be broken down on a tire machine in order to install tire rings, the results are well worth the few dollars spent. In the past few years, some dealers have started using a special technique in which they actually "paint" whitewalls on their

Tire toppers can turn blackwalls into whitewalls, cover marred whitewalls, or correct a mis-matched whitewall problem.

used cars. However, a few bumps against the curb prove that this method has its pitfalls.

If your tires already match and the whitewall portion is still in good shape, then some strong detergent and a stiff brush will make those whites stand out. For the final touch on all tires, a couple coats of ArmorAll Protectant over the entire outside surface will give them a new look.

ArmorAll Protectant also brings out the original color and sheen on items such as the rubber weatherstripping around the windows, and the rubber or vinyl inserts found on the bumpers of later model cars.

Whitewalls make a difference!

Wheel covers

ORIGINAL. I'm going to use this word many times throughout this book, so please get accustomed to seeing it. If your car is missing a hub cap or two, don't go looking for a set of cheapies to replace them with. Your nearest junk yard should have the wheel covers you're looking for. If you have a medium or full-size car which has only small hub caps rather than the full wheel covers, then I

The lack of wheel covers and whitewalls ruins the appearance of this seller's car. The average buyer wouldn't take the trouble to stop and take a closer look at it.

would suggest that you go to the wrecking yard and buy the full-size covers. Before installing the larger covers, be sure to paint the edges of the wheel rims black. If you don't, these wheel covers will not look as though they were originally installed by the factory.

Wheels on many of the compacts and sports-type cars come from the factory painted a silvery color. After a few years pass, this paint fades to a dull metal color. The best remedy for this is a can of aluminum color spray paint, which can be purchased at most any hardware or department store.

Mag wheels

If you own a family-type car which has *non-factory* mag-type wheels, it might be best to replace them with stock wheels and wheel covers. Special wheels do not come cheaply, but rarely will you be reimbursed for them. Most of the better auto dealerships waste little time removing such wheels from their trade-ins. (Naturally, this doesn't apply to sports-type cars.) If you decide to leave your mag wheels on your car, be sure that all lug bolts match and the center caps are in place.

Wheelhousings

It doesn't take too long for the wheelhousings on a new car to become mud-colored and detract from even the prettiest tires and wheel covers. Rust and corrosion can also accumulate in this area. Although this is not visible from a short distance, a prospective buyer will be only inches away from this dirt when he bends over to examine the tires. The wheelhousings needn't be pretty, but a light coat of black paint from a spray can will keep the buyer's eyes from wandering any further than the tires. If some corrosion has developed, undercoating from a spray can will usually hide this, and, at the same time, will arrest its progression.

Spray black paint over the splotches of dirt, grease, and tar which have accumulated on your car's wheelhousings. If rust or corrosion is present, spray-type undercoating will hide its existence.

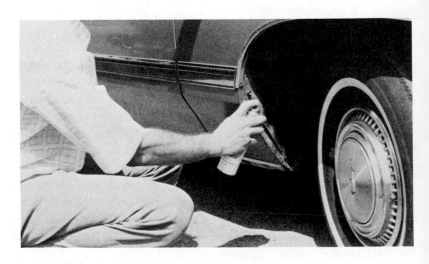

Note the texture of the undercoating which has been sprayed onto this piece of cardboard. Undercoating is great for concealing rust and corrosion inside the wheelhousings and the underside of a car. It also hides traces of body work found under the car such as fresh welds, jagged metal, etc.

Your car's body

You're probably thinking that automobile dealers have an unlimited expense account and free facilities to do body and paint work on their cars, but this isn't so. Because each car has a top price that it can bring, the dealer realizes that the fewer dollars he spends for reconditioning, the more profit he can show. Although it may seem strange to you, many dealers sublet most all of their used cars' body and paint work. The smaller, independent body shops have a much lower overhead than do the dealers, and can hire their help much cheaper.

If your car needs body work, a paint job, or both, then I suggest you go to your nearest quality used car lot and inquire as to where they have this type of work done. Get the name of the man with whom you speak, and use his name when you go to the recommended shop for an estimate. By doing this, you'll probably receive a lower price.

"It belonged to my son, who only used the back seat."

If you're not happy with the price you receive, then go to a different lot that uses a different body shop. Most professional car men are friendly and easy going, and I'm sure that you'll find one who will be more than happy to direct you to the right shop.

I once purchased from a private seller a late model El

Camino, and it needed much body work. Two other prospective buyers were at this man's home when I arrived, but when the seller showed these people repair estimates of approximately $1300, they departed. I purchased the car and had it looking like new in less than a week, spending only $600 for the repair work. The same day that it returned from the body shop, I sold it for a profit of $1200.

About painting...

If you've decided to paint your car, then try to keep it the *original* color. Not only is changing colors more costly, but the door jambs, trunk, and underpart of the hood must also be painted. If this isn't done properly, your car will look "tacky". A good paint job will cost about $90. Don't try to get a $40 or $50 paint job, because the results are usually inferior. Most of the persons to whom I sold re-painted cars weren't aware that the paint was new, and I'm proud of this fact.

Nicks and scratches. Most every parts house, hardware and department store has a shelf or rack which neatly displays small cans of touch-up paint to match almost any make or model of car. The labels on these cans suggest that touching up paint is so easy that even a child could do it. Bull. Many experienced automobile painters would not attempt to touch up a car's paint with these items. If your car has an abundance of nicks and scratches, either leave them alone or paint the entire car. Many times I have appraised automobiles on which the owners had tried to touch-up such nicks, and the small blotches of new paint looked worse than the original nicks. Whereas a polish job would've sufficed, these cars now had to be painted before I would be able to put them on the line for sale.

Moldings

Bent or missing moldings give a car a shabby appearance. Moldings are relatively inexpensive and easy to install, and are stocked by most dealer's parts departments.

Bumpers

Remove any bumper stickers with a single-edged razor blade. You can remove light rust and grime easily with chrome polish, which can be purchased almost anywhere for less than a dollar. If your license plate frames are tattered or broken, you can buy a pair of custom chrome frames for only a few dollars. A little polish on the license

An unframed or bent license plate is a great distraction.

plate itself will do no harm. (About license frames: If you own a Chevrolet, for example, then you should have frames with a Chevrolet dealer's name imprinted, or just plain chrome frames. Nothing looks more schlock than a Chevrolet with a Ford dealer's license frames.)

Lenses

All cracked or broken tail light and directional signal lenses should be replaced. Dirty lenses can be made to look new again by removing them and scrubbing both the inside and outside surfaces with a mild soap.

Glass

Cracked windshield or window glass should be replaced. If you need a new windshield, I suggest that you try to purchase a used one from a local auto glass dealer and allow him to install it. A used car dealer should be able to direct you to the right company. Also, be sure to remove all decals from your window glass.

Vinyl roofs

Vinyl roofs certainly enhance the appearance of an automobile when new, but — without proper care — can eventually become an eyesore. If your vinyl top has deteriorated to the point where it is ripped and beginning to peel, then it should be replaced. Again, ask your local used car dealer to recommend a shop to you. You should be able to have the top replaced for a price ranging from $60 to $80. If you change the color of the top, be sure that the new color compliments the interior.

When a vinyl roof is faded, discolored, or even beginning to develop a multitude of tiny cracks, a good cleaning and an application of vinyl top dressing will make it look new again. White or lighter roof covers require a good scrubbing with strong detergent to remove all of the stains.

Trailer hitches

It's unbelievable how many people try to sell their cars with trailer hitches attached. Regardless of the amount of money you paid to have a hitch installed, take it off! Even though you may have only used it once to tow a 200-pound trailer, a potential buyer will become leary

as to the condition of your car's engine and transmission, and you might easily lose a sale.

When removing a trailer hitch, do a thorough job of it. Do not let any loose electrical wires or plugs remain, as a prospect will quickly spot them.

Woodgrained exteriors

Most commonly found on station wagons, simulated woodgrain siding has a very elegant look about it when new. Unfortunately, it shares the same fate as does the vinyl top. After a couple of years of exposure to the weather and the usual lack of maintenance, it begins to lose its original luster, detracting from the car's appearance rather than adding to it.

This thin vinyl veneer is extremely expensive to replace, and very few dealers ever attempt to do so. But they have found that if the proper treatment is applied, the luster will return long enough for the car to sell. If the

The woodgrain on the left door has been treated. What a difference!

buyer continues to use a protective coating on the veneer, he will enjoy its beauty for a long while.

The best treatment I've found for this problem is a new product called, "ArmorAll Protectant." Relatively new to the market, it can be purchased in almost any major retail store in the country. It's available in a plastic spray bottle, and can be applied — with very little effort — in only a matter of minutes. The results are very good.

Under the hood

If you went to a quality used car lot and opened the hood on any of the cars, you'd probably find that the engine and its compartment sparkled as if new. Naturally, these cars don't enter the dealer's lot in this condition.

When I worked as an automobile salesman, I would have a good number of prospects look at a shining engine and tell me "I wish I could've seen it before it was cleaned". But when the occasions arose that I did show cars which hadn't yet had their engines detailed, it seemed that no one wanted to buy.

"There's rust around the radiator...Must have had cooling problems..." "Grimy looking carburetor. Probably needs and overhaul..." "Engine's awfully dirty...Must have a lot of blow-by." Remarks such as these cause dealers to waste little time in having their cars' engines detailed. ("Detailed" means thoroughly cleaned.) A prospect might gripe about a detailed engine, but will forgive it. But he might not forgive rust around the radiator, sludge surrounding the carburetor, etc. A complete engine detail at a profesional detail shop costs in the neighborhood of $18 to 25...But with about $3 and an hour's worth of work, you can attain professional looking results.

Removing engine dirt and grime

The engine should always be detailed before any painting or polishing is done to the car's exterior, because degreasing is generally a messy job. Although steam cleaning produces the best cleaning results, it sometimes removes much of the engine's paint, thus exposing bare metal and making it obvious to a buyer that dirt was just recently removed. For best all-around cleaning results, the local coin operated, do-it-yourself car wash is your best bet. The hot, high-pressured soap spray will usually remove all dirt and grease without taking the paint along with it.

Be sure to wear old clothes for this degreasing job, because you'll have to get on your hands and knees to clean the underside of your car. Before you begin cleaning, make certain that your car's engine is fully warmed-up so that its heat will dry the water you're going to spray on it. Once you've arrived at the car wash, follow these steps:

1. Remove the air cleaner and set it aside to be cleaned later.
2. Cover the carburetor openings with a plastic bag or a lint-free rag.
3. Before spraying, examine your engine closely to see where the majority of the grease and dirt has collected. Once you begin spraying, the hot water coming in contact with the hot engine will turn to steam, and will make it more difficult to see.

Be thorough! If engine is covered heavily with grime, a spray-type degreaser may have to be applied before washing.

4. Start the sprayer in the "soap" position and begin cleaning, holding the sprayer nozzle only a few inches away from the surface you wish to clean. If your car has a V6 or V8 engine, spray thoroughly under both cylinder banks. The distributor should also be sprayed, but do it quickly to prevent water from entering the distributor's interior. Wash the complete engine compartment — the inner fenders, firewall, battery, radiator, underneath side of the hood (if not covered with insulation), etc.

5. Spray the underneath side of the engine and transmission. Do a thorough job.

6. Spray the inside and outside surfaces of the air cleaner before placing it back on the engine. (Remove the filter element while spraying.)

7. Turn sprayer control to "rinse" position and remove the soap film. (It isn't necessary to rinse the car's underside.)

8. Examine the engine and its compartment carefully to insure that all dirt has been removed. If satisfied, replace the air cleaner and start the engine immediately so that its heat will dry the engine.

If, after cleaning, the engine seems to run rough, don't worry. There's probably a little moisture on the plugs or points, and the moisture will soon dry, and the engine will smooth out shortly.

From clean to sparkling

After a professional detail shop steam cleans an engine, a thin coat of lacquer is sprayed over the entire engine and its compartment. Although the sheen created by the lacquer has an artificial appearance and lasts only temporarily, it helps sell cars.

I don't recommend that an individual use lacquer, because it's messy to work with. Also, buyers expect an artificial sheen on the engines of cars being offered for sale by a dealer, but not those being offered by individual sellers.

On the other hand, the engine should have somewhat of a shine, for a clean but dull engine also looks unnatural, and the average buyer will realize that you've recently returned from the car wash.

The most inexpensive way to make your engine shine

Spray everything in sight.

without looking artificial is to apply regular motor oil to a rag and wipe the entire engine with it. (This includes all heater and radiator hoses, spark plug wires, etc.) The only drawback to using motor oil is that it has the tendency to attract dust and dirt, and the parts wiped with the oil will be greasy to the touch. For best results, I recommend ArmorAll Protectant. Spray or wipe it over *everything* under the hood. It isn't greasy, doesn't attract dust, and will bring back the engine's compartment original luster.

Wipe to a shine with a dry rag.

Before you close the hood and consider the job done, be sure that all spark plug wires are snapped into their proper place, and not laying all over the manifold. Any non-factory items such as oo-gah horns should be removed — along with the wires which leave their traces. Again — When a prospect opens your car's hood, everything should look *original*.

3

The
Interior

A major portion of this book is devoted to explaining how to repair, clean, or replace "smaller" items. A reader might at first get the impression that many of the things that I discuss are insignificant, but I tell you with all my heart that it's the "small" and supposedly "insignificant" items that make up the difference between a "sharp" car and an "edgy" car. Unfortunately, most individual sellers don't realize that if they would just spend a few dollars and replace or repair the smaller items that need replacing or repairing, and take a little time to clean the items which need cleaning, they would be able to receive a faster sale and a higher price for their cars.

Let me tell you about just one of at least fifty separate instances that I have been involved with which will illustrate this point...

It isn't an uncommon occurrence when a larger dealership has two of the same make, style, and year model of a particular car in stock. When a dealer has three or four identical models, he will generally advertise the poorest of the group in an effort to sell the others. On one occasion, the dealer for whom I worked had two 1971 Chevrolet Impala 2-doors on the used car lot when another was taken in trade on a new car. Although this most recent addition had fewer miles on it, and seemed to run better, it certainly wasn't the sharpest of the three — a couple of moldings were missing; the whitewalls were curb-scraped on one side; the vinyl top needed dressing; the paint was in need of a polish job; the interior was soiled, and the glove box door wouldn't remain shut.

Rather than spending the $75 needed to make this car ready for the front line, I decided to advertise it the way it was, and hoped to divert all prospective buyers over to the two which were sharper in appearance. The other two Impalas were priced at $2199; but, in order to attract as many prospects as possible, I advertised the newcomer for $1499 — which was only $100 over my cost.

The outcome was as expected. The car which I had advertised was shunned by those who looked at it, and the other two Impalas were sold. The following week, I spent approximately $75 to put the car which I had advertised into "front line" condition, and sold it shortly afterwards for $2199.

Although this method of advertising is referred to as the "Bait and Switch" routine, and is scorned by many, a dealer will never refuse to sell a car he has advertised, nor does he force a prospect to buy the more expensive car...The buyer makes this decision himself.

You're probably wondering why a prospect would pass up a car in need of only $75 worth of repairs, and then turn right around and buy an identical model for $700 more money. As a salesman, I had shown many of these "bait" cars, and the remarks I heard from the prospective buyers were usually the same: "I know it can be fixed cheaply, but there's just something about it that I don't like…" "The car I now have is beginning to fall apart, and I don't need another one!" "Whoever had this car

Did you know your accelerator pedal sticks?

took lousy care of it." "I'm afraid of it." "It's for my daughter. I want something nice."

"Small" items. "Insignificant" items. They create a stigma. They blow sales. This is why I must emphasize their importance.*

Upholstery Work

The vinyls and fabrics used in today's automobiles are tougher than ever, and very rarely do you see advertisements for seat covers. But some seats — especially on the driver's side — do occasionally wear or tear. At the better used car lots (the ones who receive the highest dollar for an automobile), you won't find any tears in the seats of their cars, nor will they have a car with seat covers. This certainly isn't because they only buy or take in trades which aren't in need of upholstery repair.

If a person who was unfamiliar with upholstery repair saw a car with the driver's side of the seat ripped or tattered, he would probably say the car needed seat covers. A professional automobile man looking at the same seat would say that it needed "inserting". (This means replacing only the section of the seat which is bad.) A good upholstery shop can obtain material to match that which comes from the factory, and can replace almost any section of a seat without anyone but yourself ever knowing it was replaced. If your car is in need of some seat repair, I strongly suggest that you try to retain the "original" look by having your seat inserted before ever thinking about seat covers. Although quality upholstery work doesn't come cheap, you should be able to get your money's worth by obtaining an estimate from at *least* two different shops. It's amazing how the price can vary between shops, so it's certainly worth your trouble to compare prices.

Carpeting

Only on rare occasion does carpeting wear out or tear, but − when it does − the wear is usually found in a small area which is contiguous to the "kickpad" on the driver's side. If this situation exists in your carpeting, you may be able to correct it for only a small expense. When the tear is confined to an area which extends no further than a few inches away from the factory kickpad, a good upholstery shop can sew or glue a larger kickpad which will extend *over* the original kickpad and the torn carpet at the same time.

Holes which have been burnt through the carpeting by harsh chemicals or cigarette ashes can be mended quite easily. The carpeting to patch such holes can be removed from the excess material found under the front or rear seat. The patch which you install will probably have a darker color tone, but I will tell you how to blend the colors later in this chapter.

If your carpet is worn to the point where it cannot be repaired, have it replaced at an upholstery shop with *original* carpeting. I've appraised a number of cars in which the owners have tried to dress up their car's interior with thick, bulky, bathroom-type carpeting, and it *jest don't look right!* The first thing I do when climbing behind the steering wheels of these cars is to subconsciously look around to see where they have hung the toilet tissue.

Arm Rests

If your car has an upholstered arm rest which is beginning to tear or come apart, replace it. They are usually held in place by only a couple of screws, and are easily removed. The arm rest can be re-upholstered, or you might be able to find one at your local wrecking yard. If you cannot find the correct color match, don't worry...there are many spray paints on the market that are designed specifically for vinyls, and you can change the color of the new arm rest to match the old.

Seat Mechanisms

Does your car's seat adjust easily? Before a prospect takes your car for a test drive, he (or she) will generally adjust the seat, and it's embarrassing when one must struggle to move it. This problem can be eliminated by applying a few drops of oil to the seats' tracks and latch mechanisms. If you have any knobs missing from your seat levers, replace them.

Knobs

The knob which breaks most frequently is the window crank knob. Not only does the missing knob look bad, but it also makes it awkward to roll the window up or down. New knobs — or in some case, new crank handles — can be purchased from your local dealer's parts department, and can be installed in only a matter of minutes.

Any knobs missing from your car's dashboard (radio knobs, etc.) should be replaced. *Non-factory,* custom-type knobs might look pretty to you, but not to prospective buyers. They, too, should be replaced with original equipment. (This includes gear shift lever knobs.)

Non-factory steering wheels

In the early 1960's, small, sports-type steering wheels were introduced to the market to replace the larger, bulkier wheels found on earlier model cars. Although the steering wheels used on today's automobiles aren't nearly as large or as bulky, the small, custom wheel hasn't totally lost its grip on the market.

If you have installed such a wheel on your car, it would be best to replace it with the original wheel. To simply leave the custom wheel on your car and tell the prospective buyers who look at your car that you have the original wheel if they so desire it isn't good enough...It must be replaced before anyone sees it.

Any items attached to your car which aren't going to be included in the sales price should be removed before your car is advertised. If you are removing a stereo, for example, make certain that you leave no traces of its existence. If you have cut holes in your car's doors for the speakers, then you should either replace the interior door panels, or at least leave the speaker covers in place so that no empty holes remain.

CLEANING YOUR CAR'S INTERIOR

Before a quality used car dealer offers a car for sale, he'll have its interior cleaned thoroughly. This process

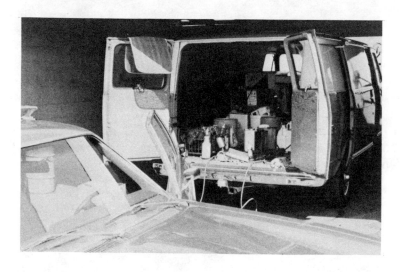

Although one would generally assume that interior cleaning is a simple procedure, the average detailer will spend over 1½ hours on each interior that he cleans. Pictured above is a van owned by an independent detailer who does his work on the dealers' premises. Special cleaning solutions, paints, and dyes are carefully applied to give interiors an "original" look.

entails more than merely vacuuming and damp-ragging, and generally takes from 1½ to 3 hours to complete. A detail shop normally charges about $30 to clean a car's interior, but you can obtain professional results by following these steps...

Add some dishsoap to a pail of warm water. Apply solution to entire dashboard, instrument panel, sun visors, and steering wheel with a large sponge.

Use a toothbrush (preferably your wife's) to remove the dirt from those spots the sponge will not reach.

Generously apply soap solution to the door panels and seats with a soft-bristled scrub brush. If your car has a cloth interior, be less generous with the soap and water. Stubborn stains in cloth can generally be removed with spot remover.

Using a stronger solution of soap and warm water, scrub carpets vigorously. Also scrub the door jambs. When finished, excess suds and moisture can be removed with a wet/dry vacuum or a towel.

Take a towel dampened with cold water and remove the soap film from the dashboard, door panels, seats, etc. Roll down your car's windows and leave its doors open and allow the interior to dry.

The professional touch

A good detail man doesn't consider his job done when he puts away the soap and water. He knows that although the car he has just cleaned may be five or six years old, it must have a fresh look about it when a potential buyer views it. Using special paints, dyes, and chemicals, he transforms the interior from clean to sparkling.

There are numerous car-care products on the market today, and, with their help, you can make your car's interior sparkle also.

Carpeting. If the carpeting in your car has begun to discolor, you can bring back its original tone by spraying it with a special fabric paint. (This paint will also hide any patches you may have inserted in your carpet earlier.) You can purchase fabric paint in spray can containers, and it can be applied quite easily. Many colors are usually available and you should be able to find the one you need — but be sure to first test the color on a small, concealed area of the carpet.

Vinyls. There are also some vinyl paints on the market which can renew sun-faded items such as dashboards, rear package trays, door panels, etc. If you have vinyl seats and have decided to apply vinyl spray paint to them,

A coat of ArmorAll Protectant produces a fresh look on the dashboard, instrument panel, steering wheel, door panels, and seats.

be sure to use a good brand. I once sold a car to a woman who loved its pretty blue seats, but was ready to tear me apart when the "pretty blue" ended up on her favorite white dress.

In most cases, the use of vinyl paints isn't necessary, for there are products available which will add a nice gloss to vinyls. Of all the products I've tried, I have found that ArmorAll Protectant produces the best natural-looking sheen on all vinyl, plastic, wood, rubber, or leather items. I mention this product by name because I know it works. The shelves in the automotive sections of most major stores are filled with car-care products, and I'd hate to see you waste your money on one that didn't give results.

Last but not least, remove all articles from your glove box and trunk which don't belong. (If you have an owner's manual, leave it in the glove box. It makes a prospective buyer feel good when he discovers it.) The only items which should be in your car's trunk is the spare tire and a jack, and make sure they're secured in their proper place. I can't count the number of times that I have looked at cars for sale in which the sellers had left motor oil, transmission fluid, tow cables, jumper cables, and so forth in their cars' trunks. Items such as these tell any potential buyer that 'ol bessy ain't so reliable.

For some strange reason, many buyers think that a clean trunk indicates a car was well-cared for. Humor them by making sure that your car's trunk is spotless. If the factory rubber mat has deteriorated, have it replaced or purchase similar material from an upholstery shop and use the old mat as the pattern.

4

Setting
Your
Price

How much should you ask for your car? How much should you be willing to accept? Since no two used cars are exactly identical in condition or color, you'll have to arrive at a price yourself. You can best arrive at this figure by using the comparative approach. How much are cars similar to yours selling for? You can answer this question by checking the automobile classified ads in your local newspapers.

Give more attention to the private sellers' ads than to the dealers. Some dealers will advertise an automobile at a very low figure for the purpose of attracting prospective buyers to their lots, but the "great buys" generally turn out to be real turkeys. If you find a few models that are more or less similar to yours, but the ads don't fully describe the cars, don't be embarrassed to telephone these sellers to obtain more details; they don't know that you're not looking to buy. Once you've arrived at the average price asked by individual sellers, compare this figure to the average price asked by automobile dealers.

Rather than telephoning the dealers, go in person to

"Alright, Alright — I'll give you what you're asking...But first you'll have to stick $300 in the glove box."

look at what they have to offer. If you telephone, the switchboard operator may connect you with a salesman who has only been in the business for a couple of weeks and knows very little about automobiles. Or your call might be answered by a salesman who is in a sarcastic mood who will be no help to you whatsoever.

When I was working as an automobile salesman, I would receive an average of two calls a day from persons wanting to sell their cars themselves. "How much should I ask?", they would question me. Naturally, without seeing their car, it was almost impossible for me to quote them a price. Although I was always patient with these callers, some of my fellow workers were not — and would sometimes humor themselves by misleading a caller. I once overheard a salesman's side of a conversation with such a caller, and it was such a classic that I have to repeat it. It went like this:

"Hello, this is the used car department, Mike speaking...You wanna know how much you can ask for your '68 Chevy van?...How many miles on it? ...Uh-huh...Six or V8?...Uh-huh...Well, pal, if it's sharp you should be able to get about $1650 for it...Yeah, really!...If it's sharp, you can expect to receive $1650 easily...Yeah, a sharp one will bring it...I wouldn't kid ya...You say it's just average? Figure $200. Good-bye."

Generally, a large dealer can sell a car — depending on the year model — for approximately $400 to $1100 more than can an individual. Why? Because he's an expert at selling cars for top dollar. Don't always expect to receive the same high price that an automobile dealer can obtain, because his price includes *services* such as arranging financing, a guarantee, the acceptance of trades, and the facilities to do the work covered by guarantees. The larger automobile dealers also spend a great amount of money advertising to attract buyers to their lots, employ used car managers to make each car look its best, and pay a fair commission to the professional automobile salesmen who are capable of selling cars for high dollars.

Many people make the mistake of asking the same

price for their car as would a dealer. After they've tried unsuccessfully for several weeks to sell it, they become panicky or disgusted and drop the price to a ridiculously low figure. Naturally, the car then sells immediately.

Try to price your car midway between the average price asked by the private parties, and the average price asked by dealers. When an individual sells his car for only $200 less than what the average dealer asks for the same automobile, he's done a good selling job. Naturally, I'm not referring to hard-to-find cars or trucks. If you have a model which is difficult to find on the lots — and it's sharp — then go ahead and ask more than a dealer would. You might get it! If you don't, you can always come down in price.

If you go to a used car lot to check prices on models comparable to yours, don't take the car you're trying to sell! Any good salesman will pay strict attention to the car which a person coming onto the lot has climbed out of. When you begin asking the prices of cars similar to yours, the salesman will get the impression that you're playing games with him and he might easily quote you the wrong prices.

Why? Because it isn't an uncommon occurrence when a prospective buyer asks the price of a car identical to the one he's driving before asking the prices of the other cars. An experienced salesman will know that this generally indicates that the prospective buyer plans to trade in his car, and is asking this question to get a general idea of what to expect for a trade-in allowance.

Naturally, there's a big difference between trade-in value and retail value, but the salesman won't want his prospect to know this. As a result, he quotes a low price on the car similar to the one being driven by his prospect.

If the salesman is ever caught mis-quoting prices, all he has to say is that he had his prices "mixed up". So again, take a different car.

When you price your car, be sure that the last two digits are 75. If you've decided, for example, to price your car at $2400, then make the price $2475. The two figures

Don't worry about mileage — I'll set the speedometer at any number you tell me

look and sound nearly identical. Do *not* end your price with a "95" or "99" as do the dealers, because it will give any potential buyer the impression you're pushing for the last dollar. Always end your price with 75. Also, never price your car at an even-thousand mark. For instance, a $2,000 price tag isn't nearly as attractive as a price of $1975.

If you receive only one or two phone calls when you advertise your car for sale, don't panic. Car sales are always up and down, even for the individuals. As a salesman, I had sold as many as five cars in one day, and in the following five days sold nothing. Fortunately, sales slumps in the used car business generally exist for only a week or two before reversing.

Competition is another obstacle that might keep your phone from ringing. During the time that I was buying and selling cars on my own, I would always look through the classified section of the newspaper before placing an ad to see what competition I would be faced with. On many occasions, when I placed the ad I saw only a few cars that would compete with mine, but the next day the classified section would have an abundance of ads that were in direct competition with my car. When this happened, all I could do was to hope that my knowledge in ad writing would pay off, and that I would receive enough phone calls so that I could convince a caller to come and see what I had to offer.

Once I went a step further. On Friday I had placed an advertisement for a Ford Galaxie which was to appear in the next morning's edition of the paper. Saturday I awoke early to check my ad, and I became irritated to see an ad for an identical model priced for only half of what I was asking for mine. I immediately went to view my competition and found it to be an excellent buy — so I bought it. I now had two Ford Galaxies, but sold them both that afternoon from my one ad. The man who purchased the Galaxie that I had bought earlier that morning commented that he had answered an ad for a car just like mine that morning, but it had been sold. "Probably junk...," I answered.

If you meet competition in the fashion that I've mentioned, keep cool. Write an effective ad, answer the callers' questions correctly, have a clean car to show, and you'll make a sale. The automobiles advertised for less than yours will either be "dogs" or be sold. Either way, your competition will be eliminated.

5

Advertising
For
Results

"Cancel my ad in your paper," I told the newspaper office.

"Your ad just came out in today's paper, Mr. Hill...Did you sell your car already?" asked the clerk.

"No...," I replied, "but after seeing my ad, I've decided it's just the car I've been looking for, and have decided to keep it."

The method in which you advertise your car is going to play an important role in obtaining the highest possible dollar for it. Although it takes little effort to telephone the local newspaper office to place an advertisement for your car, the number of calls you'll receive will hinge greatly on your ad's wording.

Rather than starting off by telling you the correct procedure for writing an effective, result-producing ad, let's first examine some advertisements in which the sellers have innocently inserted unnecessary and detrimental words.

'72 Nova 4dr. Radio, heater, 2
new tires, new alternator, and
battery. reasonable.
ph. 234-5678

Mistake #1.

Who cares about a radio and heater? Most people would assume that most every car manufactured contains these items. The seller forgot to state whether the engine is a six or eight cylinder, or if the transmission is a stick shift or automatic.

Mistake #2.

When an automobile has had one or several parts replaced, there's usually no need to mention it in the ad. When you do, the person reading it will get the impression that you're expecting to be reimbursed for all your recent expenses through the selling price.

Mistake #3.

This particular ad states that the car has two new tires. I don't know about you, but the first thing I think of is that the other two tires must be on their last mile. "How come the back two tires are red?" I asked. "Them are the inner tubes," he replied.

Mistake #4.

"Reasonable". If this seller's car is priced "reasonably", then why doesn't he come right out and state his price? This thought will go through any reader's mind, and for good reason. Every time I've phoned a "reasonable" seller for the actual price, and he quoted it, I had a strong urge to ask him if the paper may have inserted the wrong year model.

Mistake #5.
The seller, through his ad, has done nothing to make his car look enhancing.

'75 Ford LTD 2dr. Cpe. Full pwr,
Fact. Air, Lo Miles, New Trans,
Blue. Must see to appreciate.
$3999
ph. 234-5678

Mistake #1
You've probably already spotted something which doesn't look just right. A new transmission should *never* be mentioned, especially on a late model or low-mileage car. The same goes for engines, differentials, etc.

Mistake #2.
The color of a car shouldn't be brought out in an ad. If the reader doesn't particularly like the color blue, he'll pass over this ad. Because there are over 100 shades of blue, he might like it if he were to see it; but, unless he answers the ad, he'll never know.

Mistake #3.
"Must see to appreciate". This phrase implies that you might have the cleanest car in town, but at the same time it also implies that you might have the highest price in town. Don't use it.

Mistake #4.

The price $3999. This particular seller thinks that he's very clever by adding 99 to his price — just like a dealer. What other tricks are up this fellow's sleeve? Probably none, but the price can put a bad taste in a reader's mouth. It should be $3975.

'70 VW "bug". 4spd, New paint &
seat cvrs, Mag wheels $900.
        ph. 234-5678

Mistake #1.

"New paint and seat covers". The first thing I think of when I see the words "new paint" is a $29.95 paint job. The second thought that comes to my mind is Homer painting the car one Sunday in his driveway, using a paint roller, and a can of spray paint for the fine detail work. "I think we shoulda washed it before we started painting," says Homer's brother, Clovis.

"Just needs rubbin' out...," answers Homer.

The third thing I think of is "Did it have body work before it was painted?" The fourth thing that flashes through my mind is that it might be a beautiful, $200 paint job. My last thought is "Probably not...No use wasting the phone call."

Similar thoughts come to my mind with the words "seat covers". "These Mustang seat covers fit this ol' VW pretty good," says Homer.

"They'd really look good if the colors matched!" says Clovis.

"Gimme some more glue and another can of beer, Clovis," says Homer.

Mistake #2.

"Mag wheels". They might look good on the car, but not in the ad. The man looking through the newspaper for a car for his wife or daughter will pass over any car listed with sports-type equipment. If you have an automobile with special wheels, for example, and feel that they add much as to the appearance of the car, then it isn't necessary that you remove them — just don't advertise the fact. Let the prospective buyers discover them when they come to view the car. Who know? It might help make the sale.

Mistake #3.

Again, the price. It should be $875 or $975.

'74 Camero — V8, auto, Air,
V/Roof, 28,000 miles. Book:
$3320. Sacrifice! $3175.
          ph.234-5678

Mistake #1.

"Book". Never use this term, nor the terms "high book", "black book", "blue book", "wholesale value", etc. If you do, the reader will think that you're too smart to allow him to receive a good buy.

Mistake #2.

"Sacrifice". I don't believe that you can pick up the classified section of a newspaper any day of the week without finding several different sellers "sacrificing" something. (I wonder if their ancesters were pagans?)

'70 Mustang Fastback, Classic!
429V8, 4spd. Dual carbs, headers,
high-speed white ltrd. tires. Dual
glass-packs, Hvy duty clutch,
fiberglass hood. Never raced.
$3000.
ph. 234-5678

Mistake #1.

The word "classic" shows too much pride, and suggests overpricing. If the car is truly a classic, or a collector's item, the reader will usually be aware of it.

Mistake #2.

"High-speed tires". It would be much better to tell the brand name. "Heavy duty clutch" hints abuse. This type of equipment should only be discussed when a person answering the ad inquires about it.

Mistake #3.

"Never raced." Horseshit. I have the feeling that this seller speaks with a forked-tongue, and probably has some more B.S. up his sleeve.

Mistake #4.

This is one case where the price should be deleted. When the potential buyer calls for the price, the seller will have the opportunity to justify his price by describing the car in detail.

'70 Chev. Imp. V8, AT, n.trs, gd.
cond. $975.   cash only!
ph. 234-5678

Mistake #1.
This seller used too much abbreviation, and neglects to state the body style.

Mistake #2.
"Good condition". This indicates that the car is *not* in top condition, and does little to enhance it. The words "clean", "original", or "nice condition" would have a much more positive effect.

Mistake #3.
"Cash only" might insult a potential buyer enough so that he won't call. Check the credit of a buyer *after* he has committed to buy. Sure — there are a few thieves out there somewhere, but there's also some crooked sellers that the buyers must beware of. In many cases, a seller will insert the words "cash only" in his ad only to indicate that he isn't interested in taking a trade; but, since very few buyers are looking to trade; no mention should be made of it.

Well, I think these ads have shown you how to eliminate detrimental words, phrases, and prices. You're probably asking yourself "What is there left that I can use?" — Don't worry, there's plenty. Let's now take a look at some ads which have proven to be very effective...

'74 Nova LN 2 dr — 6cyl. Auto, Pwr Steering, pwr. brks, fact air, Lo miles, very clean $2975
ph. 234-5678

'65 Mustang Cpe. Small V8, Automatic, Pwr. strg, Nice cond. $1275.
ph. 234-5678

'71 Ford Maverick 4dr, 6cyl, 3spd, original owner $1275.
ph.123-4567

'73 Pontiac Ventura 2dr. cpe. — small V8, Automatic, Pwr. Strng, Factory Air. Orig. Owner, Very Pretty. $2375.
ph. 234-5678

'69 Camaro 350V8, 4 speed, original. $1475
ph. 234-5678

'68 Chev. Impala 2dr. Hdtp. Auto, Fact. Air. Looks and drives fine. $975
ph.234-5678

'72 Cadillac Cpe DeVille, Full pwr, Air, low mileage. Mama's Car $3275.
ph.234-5678

'72 Ford Co. Squire 10 pass. wgn. Full pwr, fact. air, Low mileage. Very Nice $2175.
ph. 123-4567

'66 Ford Falcon 2dr. 6cyl, Automatic, pwr. steering. Well maintained. $875.
ph.234-5678

As you see, these ads have been kept very simple and contain a minimum of abbreviations. In fact, some are so simple that it looks as though amateurs wrote them...But that's exactly the impression you should want to make.

Here are some effective words that you should try to employ when writing an ad for your automobile:

Clean, very clean, exceptionally clean, very pretty, nice, very nice, original, original owner (when applicable), looks and drives nice, "Mama's car," Daughter's car, "Grandma's car," well-kept, well maintained, well cared for, low mileage.

I believe you'll find the words which fit your car among these. You'll no doubt be tempted to be over-descriptive about your car, but please don't. *Keep your ad simple!* Also, keep the add *small*. Your ad needn't be large to attract attention. Serious buyers go through the classified section with a "fine-tooth comb", and when they run across a smaller ad which is worded attractively, they believe that they've really discovered something, and will be more apt to call.

Engine Size

With today's high fuel prices, most every automobile buyer is concerned with the amount of gas a car will consume. If the car that you're advertising has a four or six-cylinder engine, make sure that you state this fact. If it has a V8 engine which is approximately 350 cubic inches in size or less, advertise it as a *small* V8.

Choosing the paper in which to advertise.

Many people make the mistake of choosing their home-town newspaper. Naturally, if you reside in a rural community and have no choice, you'll just have to make the best of it; but, if you live in a somewhat populated area, then choose your community's most popular selling paper. If you can't decide between a couple of different papers, then call their offices and inquire as to the number of their daily, *paid* circulation. (Many newspaper publishers have papers which they distribute free-of-charge, but still count them as part of their circulation. These free papers are not as well read as are the ones which are purchased. This is why it's important to find out what amount is *paid*.)

Classified advertising is relatively inexpensive, so don't use an inferior paper merely to save a dollar or two...or you'll be stepping over dollars to pick up pennies. In order to obtain the fastest sale possible, I'd suggest you use two papers.

Live in a rural community?

Do you have close friends or relatives living in a larger city? You might consider spending a Saturday or Sunday with them, and borrow the use of their phone for the day

And if it ain't exactly like I tell you, you can come back and call me a jack ass.

to receive calls from an ad placed in their area's newspaper. If you're able to do this, and plan to visit on a Saturday, for example, start the ad on a Thursday, and have it run through Saturday. I think that the visit could prove to be very profitable.

What day to advertise?

It's a known fact that more people will look for an automobile on a Friday, Saturday, or Sunday...But automobile ads usually abound on these days, and the competition is much greater. This doesn't mean you should bypass week-end advertising, but you shouldn't overlook the early part of the week when ads are few.

When I advertise to sell a car, I usually have the ad start on a Thursday and run through the following Monday. (Note: Unless absolutely necessary, avoid inserting the time in which you wish the buyer to call because it will detract from your car. If no one is at your home to answer phone calls during the day, the prospective purchaser will call back.)

A good ad alone will not sell an automobile. Its main purpose is to induce as many prospective buyers possible to lift up the receiver on their phone and dial your number...The more people that call, the better chance you have of making a sale and receiving your price!

6

When The Phone Rings

Your car is ready to go, and you've placed your ad in the newspaper. What questions will be asked? What are the best answers? Let's take a look at the touchy ones...

"How many miles are on the car?"
This is the most common question you'll be asked. If your automobile has higher than average mileage and you've done some major work on it, then this is the time to tell about it. If the miles are mostly "highway" miles, relay this information to the caller, also. If there are 80,000 miles on your car, for example, and it looks as though it has 30,000 miles on it, tell the caller this! (A quick word about mileage: There's always conversation about the large number of persons who turn the speedometers back on their cars. Actually, very little of this takes place. Not only is this practice illegal, but it's morally wrong. There's a big difference between "horse-trading" and lying. *(P.S. — It will also burn up your drill motor.)*

"What shape is the car in mechanically?"

The best answer for this is: "It's very reliable." When questioned further, don't try to play mechanic. If you're not a mechanical genius, then tell the caller this.

On many, many, different occasions I've run into peo-

Can you back it up to the phone and race the engine?

ple selling automobiles for a song because they thought that it had a major mechanical problem. Half of the time they had concluded this on their own, and the other half of the time some backyard mechanic had convinced them of it.

I'll never forget the time I answered an ad for a Ford Falcon...The ad stated "needs engine". When I met the seller, he told me that he had a new engine installed less than six months earlier, but it had "thrown" a connecting rod. I was able to start the car, and immediately recognized the loud banging noise as a sticking valve. I paid the man $50 for it, took it home and worked on it for less than one hour, and the problem was cured. One week later I sold it for $400.

In a similar case, I bought a beautiful Ford Fairlane which had a terrible bearing noise, and the oil light wouldn't go out. This seller was convinced that his car's engine was worn out. When I removed the oil pan, I discovered that the oil pump's screen was dirty and was restricting the flow of oil. I cleaned the screen, put it back together, and it ran like a top. Three days later, I sold the car for three times what I had paid for it.

I can go on and on, but I believe these examples will put the point across. The people who will answer your ad will not expect you to be a mechanic, so don't try.

"How's the body?"

I don't believe that there are too many cars around which don't have a fair share of nicks in the paint, especially along their sides. In the automobile selling profession, these nicks are known as "shopping cart rash". You can guess how the dealers arrived at this name. Most buyers will forgive it.

If your car has a sizable dent on its body and you haven't gone to the trouble or expense of having it repaired, then at least obtain some written estimates. Most people have unsubstantiated opinions about the cost of body work. When you tell your callers that your car has a dent in the front fender, for example, you can imagine what's going through their mind; but, you can calm down their imagination when you tell them that you have a written estimate for under $65.

When you're selling a car which has new paint and the caller asks about the condition of the paint, don't mention the fact that the paint is new. Simply say it's "very nice". The same applies to seat covers.

"Did you buy the car new?"

If you own a later-model car, then expect this question from about 60% of the callers. Naturally, if you did purchase it new, you can say "yes". If you didn't, then simply say "no", without going into detail. If you've owned the automobile for only a short time, then don't volunteer this information.

Another tip — If you purchased a demonstrator from a dealer, you can state that you're the original owner. Although an automobile dealer may use a car for a period of time, it usually isn't first registered until sold.

The best reason to avoid mentioning that your car was purchased as a "demo" is because of the misunderstanding most people have of the term. A demo is *not* an automobile used solely for the purpose of giving demonstration rides to prospective buyers. In fact, these "demos" are generally assigned to only one person — usually a salesman, sales manager, office manager, service manager, or the dealership owner himself.

The dealers receive a fair "demo allowance" from the manufacturer, so they take full advantage of this by tagging many of their executives' cars as "demos". The dealers, in most cases, give these automobiles much better care than would an individual.

"Will you take less than what you're asking?"

Some callers will ask this question, so you must be prepared with an answer. Even though you might consider accepting a lower price, don't make any type of commitment to the person who is calling, and don't ever feel that you are obligated to do so. I would recommend that you word your response like this...

"Well, gosh...I don't know...Will you pay me *more*

Very reliable — I use it every day.

than what I'm asking?" Say this in a pleasant, joking, manner. The caller will generally laugh or stutter for a moment, and you should continue by saying: "Please let me tell you my address so that you can come and see the car, and then you can decide whether or not you're even interested, o.k.?"

7

The
Easy Sell

Before we meet the buyers, let's set the stage. First, be sure that your home — at least the exterior — looks its best. The yard should be trim and tidy. If you went to an automobile dealership and noticed the lot was unkempt, wouldn't you be leary of their used automobiles? This applies even more so to individual sellers.

During my car-buying career, I would always pay strict attention to the premises when I arrived at the sellers' homes. I knew that when a home was well-maintained, I stood a very good chance of finding a well-maintained automobile — and, of course, visa versa. If a seller's yard was messy and his car was clean, I would look it over pretty darn carefully. "Not like this guy to have a clean car," I thought.

I'm not suggesting that you need a home that looks as if it belongs in "Better Homes and Gardens", but it should be at its best.

This seller's car would look much more attractive if only he would mow his lawn.

After you've received a few phone calls and know that you will have some prospective buyers arriving soon, go to your car and run the engine long enough for it to warm up. Everybody starts a car differently, so there's a much better chance that your car will start immediately — for anybody — when the engine is somewhat warm. Also, engines in some automobiles have loud tappet noises when cold. Although such noises may be nothing serious, they can easily queer a sale. Every automobile dealer has his used cars started and warmed up every morning for this reason. When a good automobile salesman knows that he has a customer coming to the lot to look at a particular car, he will drive it around the block a few times to help eliminate any chances of trouble.

"For Sale" signs

Be sure to remove any "For Sale" signs from your car. When someone answers an advertisement, they'd like to believe that they're one of the first persons who view your car...But if they see a sun-faded "For Sale" sign in the rear window, they'll feel as though they're looking at merchandise which has been on the shelf for a long time. When you remove your sign, do a thorough job! A square, yellowed frame of scotch tape will have the same detrimental effect as will the sign itself.

Greeting the prospective buyer.

How do you picture a successful, professional, automobile salesman? Do you envision a fast-talking, aggressive type of person? Well, very seldom is he fast talking, and although he's usually aggressive, he probably won't let his prospective buyers know it. I tell you now that the automobile salesman who consistently makes excellent wages for himself is calm and collective. He doesn't *sell* cars, but instead helps his customers *buy*. He does this by wisely wording his conversation with them.

I've dealt with hundreds of private sellers, and I have found that a good percentage of them believe that they must talk fast and hard — like they believe a car salesman would do in order to make a sale. Well, a fast-talking, private-party seller is more obnoxious than a fast-talking automobile salesman. If you want to receive top dollar for your car, you'll have to forget about any fast talking.

When you greet a prospective purchaser, be friendly — But do as little talking as possible. If you think you have the most beautiful car in town, keep these thoughts to yourself. You needn't tell someone that a car is sharp...They'll see this for themselves. Act humble, but slip in a few seemingly innocent words into your conversation. For example: When a prospective buyer asks to drive you car, say "Certainly...but please don't be gone for more than a few minutes...I have others coming to see

Practice these expressions

the car." This remark contains no bragging, but it certainly contains some selling. (Unrecognized by the buyer, of course.)

Now let's take a look at the remarks you will hear, the questions you'll be asked, and the answer you should have ready for the prospective purchasers....

"I see that you've really cleaned up the outside of the engine — I wish I could've seen it before it was cleaned."
This remark will come from about 40% of the persons looking at your car. It will usually be in a sarcastic tone, and the prospect will be very proud of being so clever as to notice it. You answer, "I'm sorry, but I've always kept my engine clean so that I would be able to recognize anything wrong developing..." If the buyer raises an eyebrow at your answer, give him an angelic look.

"May I take the car to my mechanic?"
"Yes! Absolutely!...But I'm afraid I can't let you take it today or tomorrow, because I'm expecting more people who are coming to see the car." Don't worry. Declining to allow your car to be viewed immediately by a buyer's mechanic will not hinder your chances of making a sale in the least, as long as you have happily agreed to let the prospect show it to him a few days later. In most cases, a prospective buyer will ask this question only to see what your response will be. With the response I've suggested, you'll accomplish two things: (1) Ease the buyer's mind about the mechanical condition of your car by agreeing to let him take the car to his mechanic; (2) Suggested — without actually speaking the words — that if he's serious about buying your car, he'd better do it before somebody else does.

About "mechanics" and "advisors"...
If you have an automobile which is in tip-top mechanical condition, you'll probably see no reason why you should avoid allowing a prospective buyer take it to his mechanic or advisor. But let me relate to you just a few of my many, many, poor experiences with the same...

Incident #83...

On one occasion, I permitted a prospect to take a nice, low-mileage Nova 4-door to his local service station mechanic. I didn't want to take the time to go along with the prospect, so I let him go alone. Although he said he'd only be gone for about 30 minutes, he didn't return until almost two hours had passed. The prospect apologized for being gone for such a long time, and then stated he would have to decline purchasing my car. "What kind of a mechanic did you take it to?!" I jumped. "My car is in excellent condition!"

"Oh, my mechanic says that your car is definitely in good shape...," said the prospect, "But he told me about a friend of his that had a 2-door Nova in the same condition for the same price. He called his friend and had him bring the car to his station, and I bought it. I feel kinda bad about not buying your car, but a 2-door was just what I really wanted..."

Then my prospect went into great detail about his new purchase, describing the color, the care it had had, and so forth. I believe that he wanted me to share in his new-found joy, but I wasn't in the celebrating mood at the present time. I blew it. I'm sure that if I would have gone along, the mechanic would've kept his thoughts to himself, and I would have made the sale.

Incident #27...

I had purchased a 14' commercial-type step van. (This looks like a bread van, the type in which you stand while driving.) I paid $600 for it, and advertised it the following week for $1375, which it was well-worth. A young man that was looking for a truck such as this to convert into a camper answered my ad, and was pleased with what he saw. He had cash-in-fist, and was more or less committed to buy...But first he wanted to drive it. "Fine," I said. "I'll go along with you."

He drove the truck on a nearby freeway for about ten miles, and then chose a large boulevard for the return trip back to my home. The truck ran like a top, and I knew I had a sale.

Approximately one mile from my home, the young man asked if he might be allowed to make a quick stop to show it to his stepfather. "Certainly," I said proudly. I knew it was in the best mechanical condition, and had nothing to worry about — I thought.

Well, he soon pulled the truck over to the curb in front of a small beer tavern, and went inside to find his step-dad. "Oh-oh..." I thought. "What have I gotten myself into this time?" A few moments passed, and out came the stepfather — half crocked.

"Good morning," I said, putting on my angelic smile.

"Hmmphh!" he answered. "How's it drive, son?"

"Great, dad. I took it for quite a long drive on the freeway."

"Son, what you need to do is take it on about a 500-mile trip before you buy it. That's the only way you can know its condition for sure..."

"Gee, dad, I never thought of that."

"That's what I'm here for, son...How much is he asking for this thing?"

"$1375, dad."

"Well, son, take it to a truck dealer and ask them what they'll give you for it wholesale, then offer this man that amount."

I was becoming nauseous, and I could see my $775 profit disolving away. I knew that I had to get this young man away from his step-dad before anything could develop, so I motioned him into the truck and headed for home.

"My step-dad's quite a guy..." he said. "I always go to him for good advice." Well, I said everything I could to repute his stepfather's suggestions, but it was evident that this young man wasn't going to buy anything from me. (I refer to this fellow as a "young man", but he was about 26 years old, three years older than I was at the time.)

"How's about we stop and get some milquetoast at this corner restaurant?" I asked in a biting tone.

Not catching my intended insult, he answered: "No, tomorrow's my step-dad's birthday, and I have to go and find a present for him this morning." I was thinking of suggesting that he buy his step-dad a one-piece puzzle, but figuring he'd probably have great difficulty with it, I kept my mouth shut. I pulled the truck into my driveway, and the young man climbed out and departed — along with his money.

Incident #37...

I had a very clean Chevrolet Malibu 2-door which had a smooth-running, six-cylinder engine. A minister from a nearby church came to view the car and after driving it decided to purchase it, providing his mechanic approved. The car was low mileage, so I didn't anticipate any problems.

After driving a short distance, we arrived at the mechanic's place of business...an old, dilapidated, single-car garage which sat behind a small frame house. The mechanic appeared to be in his late sixties, wore an old pair of faded blue overalls, and moved with the speed of a snail. Climbing out of the car, I noticed that his garage was well equipped. He had pliers and pipe wrenches to fit every make and model of car, and he even had metric pliers and screwdrivers for the imports. "Maybe he's a good ol' boy," I thought.

The old man lifted the hood and began removing plug wires one by one while the engine was running. "He's a God-fearing man," the minister whispered to me as we stood back, watching.

Sixty seconds passed, the mechanic closed the hood, and said "Bad compression in two of the cylinders."

"Can you please verify that with a compression gauge?" I asked.

"Don't need to..." he answered.

"Please do the car justice and drive it," I said.

"Don't need to..." was his reply. He then turned to the minister and said, "I never liked six-cylinders...You should look for a car with a V8 engine."

As the minister and I drove back to my home, I expressed my feelings. I asked that he allow me to check the compression with a gauge, and get back to him in a few hours with the results. "My mechanic's a God-fearing man," he said. "He's probably right, but you can call me if you wish."

I wasted no time taking the compression check, and, as I had anticipated, the compression was excellent in all cylinders. When I called the minister and informed him of the results, he expressed no interest in the car whatsoever. "My mechanic's a God-fearing man, and I'll have to make my decision based on his conclusions." Continuing, he said: "You say the compression is good, and maybe you're right. Just remember that you must pay for your sins when you die."

"I'm paying cash," I replied.

I could tell you about numerous instances such as

these last few, but I'm sure you get the picture. When a mechanic or advisor is a friend or relative of the prospective purchaser, he will many times let his own personal feelings and prejudices take precedent over the actual condition of the car.

Keep the windows up 'til we're away from my house — the neighbors think I have air conditioning

"May I drive the car for a couple of hours?"

When a prospective buyer asks this question, politely turn him down. Many automobile dealers allow this in order to prevent losing a prospect, but it usually does more harm than good. A potential buyer will normally get "buyer's remorse" before he's actually purchased the automobile. Although your car may be in perfect condition, the prospect will usually complain about the seat becoming uncomfortable after an hour's driving, the car not riding just right, the excessive consumption of gas, or one of a hundred other thin excuses. A short drive on a highway will be all that's necessary to show your prospect what shape your car is in.

Always go along with your prospect when he is test driving your car. It's a fact that everyone always wants to show his new purchase to a friend or neighbor. They're thinking about this when they make their decision to buy...But if they go to show the car off before they buy, (which they can very easily do if you're not along with them) then this show-off element is taken away from your package, and will hinder your chances of making a sale. Also, their friend or neighbor may pick your car apart (sometimes out of simple jealousy) and your sale will be altogether lost. REMEMBER: 1. Short drive. 2. You go along. 3. No unnecessary stops.

The prospect that picks your car apart...

I think the greatest insult that I ever experienced was when a man in his late forties came to view an old, beat-up Buick for which I was asking $400. After walking slowly around the car, he looked up at me and asked: "Anyone hurt?"

When a prospective buyer doesn't like the car he's looking at, or doesn't want it, he will usually thank you for your time and leave. The person who drives the car and stays around to pick it apart is generally the one who is interested. The prospect's down-grading of your car may only be a sham to prompt you to drop your price. I've had many an amateur bargainer verbally tear my car apart, telling me of the things that were wrong with it, all the money that would have to be spent repairing it, etc., then in their next breath offer to buy the car for a lower price. This is a very poor method of chiseling for a price reduction, because it will upset most sellers. But don't allow it to upset you.

It has been my experience that when a person offers a lower price after downgrading the car, the price he offers is usually all that he can afford...But in order to avoid embarrassing himself by telling you this, the prospect tries to convince you that the price he's offered is all that your car is worth! Here's how to handle this type of buyer...

Let's assume, for example, that you have a car which you've advertised for $1975. A prospect picks the car apart, and then offers to buy it for $1700. If this figure tempts you, don't be too quick to jump at it. Even though the prospect may only have $1700 at the present time, there's a way to get *more*. Respond to the offer along these lines..."Bob, you're the first person who has had the opportunity to see my car, and my phone has been ringing all morning. I have many other persons coming to see it. Bob, I realize that my car isn't perfect, but that's because it's a used car. But then again, I think that it's in very good condition for a car of its age. I believe that if I were to advertise it for a couple of continuous weeks, I could get more than what I've already priced it at, so I really can't accept $1700 for the car...But I'd be happy to work with you if you want the car, because I believe that you'd be happy with it. If you want to buy my car for $1975, I'd be willing to let you take delivery for $1700, and wait a few weeks for the balance."

Now wait for your prospect to speak. More than likely, he will come back at you with a counter-offer. If he does, then you should come back at him with a counter-offer to his counter-offer, until you're satisfied with the amount you'll be receiving.

How to help guarantee yourself that you'll be paid the balance...

By agreeing to finance part of the selling price for your buyer, you can receive the top dollar that you want for your car...But you must take certain precautions to avoid getting stuck. *Never* should you agree to finance any more than the difference between the competitive price and the top price. For example, if you have a car that would sell fairly easily for $1500, then there's no need to finance any part of this amount, but only that amount over $1500. (If you have a buyer who agrees to pay you $1750, for example, then the most you would carry would be $250.)

The best assurance you can have for getting paid is to retain the certificate of title until the balance is received. Since most states require that the new owner register the vehicle in his name within ten days of purchase, the buyer should agree to pay you the balance within this length of time. If he is unable to do so, then it would be best to go ahead and register the car in the new owner's name, but to show yourself as the legal owner until such balance is paid.

If you want to avoid going through this paperwork, I suggest that you accept a check for the amount that you wish to carry, and hold the check until the date that the buyer has agreed to pay the balance. If the balance is to be paid in installments, have the buyer make out a check for each installment before he takes actual delivery of the car, then deposit each check when the installment is due. (Do not accept post-dated checks. The checks should be dated the same day in which they are given, even though they may not have funds in the bank to cover them. If the buyer raises his eyebrows to this method, merely tell him: "Bob, I won't deposit them until the days we have agreed upon...Why would I want to deposit a bad check?") I've never had a buyer refuse to honor this request.

NEVER accept a promise alone to be paid. I don't mean to sound like an untrusting, cold-hearted scrooge, but I've lost too many dollars by taking a stranger's promise to pay. If the buyer doesn't have a checking account, find another buyer.

"Let me leave you a deposit..."

You'll have to use your own judgement when accepting a deposit from an interested party, but let me give you a few tips on this...

1. Never accept a small deposit. ($5, $10, $20, etc.)

2. The deposit should be *non-refundable*. Both time and money are spent when you place your ad in the newspaper. When a deposit is taken, you will have to tell all of the following prospects who telephone that your car is sold. If the person giving you the deposit has a change of heart about his purchase, you lose not only the cost of the advertisement and your valuable time, but you may also have lost the chance of selling the car to someone else.

I remember one weekend when I was in my prime as an automobile salesman, that I took five deposits on five different used cars. The following Monday, when these deals were to be completed, in came four of these buyers — one at a time — to tell me that they had to cancel their purchases. The first man told me that his brother was seriously injured in an out-of-state automobile accident, and that he had to fly back there to take care of his brother's family. "What about your job?," I asked.

"Gonna take a leave of absence for a month," he said. "I have to help my brother's family...he'd do the same for me. Mr. Hill, I need my deposit back to help pay for my trip."

Well, I knew this fellow was putting me on, but I thought "what the hell..." and gave him back his money .

The next person wanting money back was a woman in her late thirties. "Mr. Hill, I'm afraid that I can't go through with the purchase. I just found out last night that my mother, a widow, needs an eye operation, and she doesn't have any money. I want to buy the car very badly, but my family comes first...That's just the type of person I am."

Needless to say, the next two stories were similar. Each person had a sob story and had cast himself in the role as the hero. Two days later I saw the woman who was supposed to be paying for her mother's eye operation driving a new car. I suspected that all four had a new purchase in their garage. But at last I've learned how to tell when persons wanting their deposits back are telling me lies — their lips move.

3. When a person offers a deposit, don't be so quick to accept it. When a prospect gives you a deposit, he knows that he isn't committed one hundred per cent, and he might spend the next day or two trying to find a better car at a better price. Take a negative approach on deposits. Let the prospect think that your car is a real bargain. "Bob, I don't want to take a deposit from you unless you are certain that you want the car. I've had many phone

calls and expect many others to come look at it. This is a very nice car, and it's priced right. If you want the car, then I'll accept a non-refundable deposit. But I don't want it unless you're sincere." (When you use the word *"sincere"*, the buyer will prove himself *insincere* if he does *not* give you a deposit. You'll get your non-refundable deposit 99% of the time by using this wording, and the buyer will not go out and try to beat your deal in the meantime.) This negative approach will always get the job done, because it makes the prospect think that you have something extra-special for sale.

Credit Unions and banks.

If you're selling a later-model automobile, then here's a problem you might run across...

Many people make the mistake of assuming that the man who writes the advertisements for the banks is the same fellow who makes the loans. Believing this, a prospect might give you a deposit on your car — in good faith — and go to visit his old friend the banker.

The first thing the banker will do before he considers making the loan will be to make the borrower prove that he doesn't need the money. The banker's next step will usually be to pull out his "blue book" or "wholesale guide" to determine the wholesale value of the car the borrower is trying to purchase. "Gee, Bob...", says the banker. "We can only lend you $2900 on the car you're buying. How much did you say the seller was asking?"

"$3375", says Bob.

"You'll need to come up with $475", says the banker.

Now Bob only has $200, so he comes back to you and says "My banker says your car is only worth $3100." I'm afraid that ol' Bob is lying, but only because he has too much pride to admit he is short $275.

Without suggesting to Bob that you don't believe his story, you can answer him like this... "Bob, I'm sure that your banker knows plenty about finance, but is he also a professional automobile man? I'm sure that in your heart you feel that my car is priced competitively. I don't know

You'll need a co-signer for your co-signer.

you very well, but you certainly don't impress me as the type of man that lets his banker make his decisions." (By saying this, we're making Bob's pride work *for* us, and not against.) Continue your conversation along these lines... "If your banker will not lend you the full price on the car, I think I can help you out. How much is the bank willing to lend?"

Once you bring the true problem out into the open (without insulting the buyer), there will be a good line of communication. If the amount of money that the buyer is short isn't too high a figure, then it might we wise to carry this small balance yourself for a short while. Since a bank or credit union will be the one that is to be shown as the legal owner on the certificate of title, you won't be able to use it as the collateral. The best form of security is to hold the buyer's check or checks as described earlier in this chapter.

A FEW FINAL TIPS.

Protect yourself

When you decide to sell your automobile, don't wait until the last minute to find out what type of papers need to be signed. Because every state has different systems and different forms, I ask that you consult your local motor vehicle department to acquire the forms you'll need. (I hope that your state's motor vehicle department isn't as obnoxious as is mine. I once stood in line 45 minutes, and when I finally got up to the window, the 60-year-old female clerk was terribly rude to me. I lost my temper and told her to "kiss my rear". She said I'd have to go to window #8 for this.) *Always* obtain the buyer's name and address in case some problem should arise at a later date.

When a buyer is giving you a personal check for your car, call his bank and verify the funds. If this isn't possible, then do *not* release the certificate of title until the check clears. When you know that the check is good, and the bank is located not too far away, then I'd suggest that you take it there and cash it as fast as possible rather than depositing it and waiting three or four days for it to clear.

When I was 16 years old, my father had a later-model, clean, low mileage Mercury Comet station wagon. He

placed an ad in the newspaper, and the next night a man
came — along with his "mechanic" — to view the car.
After trying it out for about 30 minutes, he sat down and
haggled price with my father for about fifteen minutes.
When a price was agreed upon, he gave my father a
check, and my father gave him the certificate of title. As
the two men drove away with the car, my father commented on what nice guys they were. "Do you think the
check is good?", I asked.

"Hell," he said, "I've lived long enough to know an
honest face when I see one." He seemed a little irritated
at my lack of faith in people, so I didn't press the matter.

A week later the check came back from the bank
marked "insufficient funds." "Probably a simple mistake," said dad. "I'll put it through again." The following
week the check came back again, only this time "account
closed" was marked upon it. When dad called the buyer's
supposed residence, he got a recording saying that the
number had been disconnected. His next step was to call
the Los Angeles Police Department.

While he was explaining his problems to them, he
glanced up and saw me smirking. When his eyes met
mine, I had the feeling that I had better leave the room in
order to save him the trouble of having to also report a
murder.

The next day a detective came to our home carrying a
large notebook. Opening the first page, dad spotted the
pictures of his "honest buyer" and his "mechanic". The
next several pages were filled with checks, just like the
one dear old dad had.

"Since you signed the title over to this guy, I doubt
you'll ever see your car again. He's probably already
wholesaled it to an unsuspecting car dealer. Since the car

dealer receives the car in good faith, along with a legitimate title, he has a rightful and legal claim to the car. You shouldn't have given up the title so quickly," said the detective.

They say that experience is the best teacher, but this is one tuition that most of us cannot afford. The chances of you meeting up with a fellow like this are very slim, but I couldn't finish this book without warning you of the possibility.

How to park your car.

You're probably thinking to yourself "What's this guy doing telling me how to park my car? He must be nuts!" Believe me, I've lost plenty of sales simply because the car I was showing was parked in an awkward position. Although you may have no difficulty maneuvering your car, you have to remember that the car will handle completely foreign to the prospects who drive it...especially the females.

The most difficult thing for a woman to do in a strange car is to back up. Knowing this, park your car in a position that will not require this feat. This is especially important if your automobile is a stick shift, or does not have power steering. "This car is going to be hard on my wife without power steering...," the man told me as we turned the corner in a car I was trying to sell.

"It's good exercise," I answered. "And it will probably build her chest up two bra sizes..."

"I'll take it," he answered.

Demonstrate those small cars!

Many people today are switching from big, luxurious, gas-eating cars to the very small compacts. The number-one question that these buyers have in their minds is "How will this small car perform?" When these prospects get behind the wheel of a stranger's car, they are not about to put their question to a test, so you'll have to do it for them.

What do you think of the power?.

When they are ready to take a ride in your car, tell them that you'll drive for the first few blocks...Then give it hell! This is extremely important. I don't mean to imply that you drive like a maniac, but you must show your prospect that the car has the power to get on the freeway at a reasonable speed. I was employed at a Chevrolet dealer when the Chevette was introduced, and although many people came to see these new cars, there was only one salesman that was making any sales. This was because he was the *only* salesman that was putting himself behind the wheel during the first part of the demonstration ride.

FINAL TIP: DON'T LEAVE THIS BOOK ON THE FRONT SEAT OF YOUR CAR!

> *Thank you for buying my book. I hope that your investment is returned a hundredfold.*